History of Britain

Modern Britain

1901 to the 1990s

Andrew Langley

HAMLYN

HISTORY OF BRITAIN – MODERN BRITAIN
was produced for Hamlyn Children's Books
by Lionheart Books, London.

Editor: Lionel Bender
Designer: Ben White
Picture Researcher: Jennie Karrach
Media Conversion and Typesetting: Peter MacDonald

Educational Consultant: Jane Shuter
Editorial Advisors: Andrew Farrow, Paul Shuter

Production Controller: Linda Spillane
Managing Editor: David Riley

First Published in Great Britain in 1994
by Hamlyn Children's Books,
an imprint of Reed Children's Books,
Michelin House, 81 Fulham Road, London SW3 6RB,
and Auckland, Melbourne, Singapore and Toronto.

Copyright © 1994 Reed International Books Limited.

ISBN 0 600 582124 HB   ISBN 0 600 582132 PB

British Library Cataloguing-in-Publication Data.
A catalogue record for this book is available
from the British Library.

Acknowledgements
Picture credits Page 6: Mary Evans Picture Library. Page 7: The Mansell
Collection. Pages 8 (left), 8 (right), 9: Mary Evans Picture Library. Page
10: The Mansell Collection. Page 11: Popperfoto. Pages 12, 13, 14:
Mary Evans Picture Library. Page 15, 17 (top): Popperfoto. Page 17
(bottom): The Mansell Collection. Page 18: Pat Charlesworth/
Architectural Association. Page 20: The Mansell Collection. Page 21
(top): Robert Opie. Page 21 (bottom): The Hulton-Deutsch Collection.
Page 22: Robert Opie. Page 23 (top): Popperfoto. Page 23 (bottom), 24:
The Mansell Collection. Page 25, 26: Popperfoto. Page 27: Mary Evans
Picture Library. Page 28 (bottom): Popperfoto. Pages 28-29: The
Hulton-Deutsch Collection. Page 29: Robert Opie. Page 30: The Hulton-
Deutsch Collection. Page 31: Popperfoto. Page 32: A. Bruce/Barnaby's
Picture Library. Page 33 (left and right): Popperfoto. Page 34 (left):
Barnaby's Picture Library. Page 34 (right): Robert Opie. Page 35: Mary
Evans Picture Library. Page 36 (bottom), 37: Popperfoto. Pages 36-37:
Syndication International Ltd. Pages 38-39: Rex Features/ITN. Page 39:
Popperfoto. Page 40: Cummings/Sunday Express Newspapers. Pages
40-41: Simon Hazelgrove/Select. Page 41 (top): Popperfoto. Page 41
(bottom): Gaskill/Sunday Times/Times Media Ltd., Johannesburg.
Cover: National Trust Photographic Library/Derrick E. Witty (Churchill);
Robert Opie (ration books); Mary Evans Picture Library (omnibus);
Popperfoto (World Cup winners).
Artwork credits Stefan Chabluk: map page 4. John James: 1, 4, 6/7,
8/9, 12/13, 18/19, 20/21, 30/31, 32/33, 36/37, 38/39, 46. Mark
Bergin: 2, 5, 10/11, 22/23, 26/26, 34/35. James Field: 14/15, 16/17,
24/25, 29. Malcolm Smythe: 42/43, 45. Hayward Art: page 44 and
small maps.
Cover: Design by Peter Bennett, Artwork by Stephen Conlin.

CONTENTS

Modern Britain

During modern times there have been many changes in politics and social life which have shaped the way we live today. The photographs in this book are mostly of buildings and objects from recent events.

The illustrations in this book are based on historical evidence. They have been painted by artists who have used drawings, photographs and descriptions from the past to help them to decide how things would have looked then.

ROMAN BRITAIN 55BC to AD406	SAXONS AND VIKINGS 406 to 1066	MEDIEVAL BRITAIN 1066 to 1485	THE TUDORS 1485 to 1603	THE STUARTS 1603 to 1714	GEORGIAN BRITAIN 1714 to 1837	VICTORIAN BRITAIN 1837 to 1901	MODERN BRITAIN 1901 to the 1990s

ABOUT THIS BOOK

This book considers the Modern period chronologically, meaning that events are described in the order in which they happened, from 1901 to the present day. Some of the double-page articles deal with a particular part of modern history. Those that deal with aspects of everyday life, such as trade, houses and pastimes, are more general and cover a broader timescale. The little illustrations at the top of the left-hand pages of the articles show, in chronological order, major scientific developments, discoveries and inventions of modern times in Britain. Unfamiliar words are explained in the glossary on page 46.

About the map

This shows the location of places mentioned in the text. Some are major cities, others towns or the sites of famous buildings or events.

MAP OF BRITAIN

THE SHETLANDS

SCOTLAND

NORTH SEA

Jarrow

Derry City

Belfast

Armagh

Newry

Dundalk

IRELAND

York

Dublin

Liverpool

Skegness

ENGLAND

Sandringham

Birmingham

WALES

Coventry

Woburn Park

Stevenage

Harrow London

Buckingham Palace

Windsor

Croydon

Bristol

Aldermaston

Ascot

Epsom

Southampton

Goodwood

Portsmouth

ENGLISH CHANNEL

FRANCE

INTRODUCTION

In 1901, Britain was one of the strongest nations in the world. Her huge Empire included Canada, India, Australia and large parts of Africa. It was protected by a well-trained army and a navy which seemed unbeatable. British coal, steel and cloth were being bought all over the world. Many of its manufacturers and traders had grown very rich.

Yet, during the 20th century, life changed quickly. By the 1990s the British Empire was gone and Britain was drawn more deeply into European affairs. The armed forces had shrunk. British industry lost its dominant position in the world, too, and many factories and mines had closed forever. Britain was still a major world power, but it would never be as strong as before.

This fall was partly caused by the two world wars. These were the most important events of the age. In the First World War (1914 to 1918), over 750,000 Britons were killed. In the Second World War (1939 to 1945), over 420,000 soldiers died. Besides this, 60,000 civilians were killed in Britain by German air raids. Britain ended up on the winning side, but the wars left her weakened and massively in debt. Speeding up the decline were a growth of industry in eastern Europe, Asia and the Far East, and economic and political disasters in the United States, with which Britain traded heavily.

Since the wars, however, some things have changed for the better. Daily life for most people is much more comfortable. In 1993, nearly all British homes had running water, bathrooms, electricity and heating. Cars, televisions, washing machines and refrigerators are no longer thought of as luxuries. Many families own them all. People are also better educated, healthier and longer lived, thanks to state schools and a free health service.

EDWARDIAN BRITAIN

Edward VII was 59 years old when he became king in 1901. He was very different from his stern mother, Victoria. He loved horseracing, food and pretty women. This made him popular. "He wasn't clever, but he always did the right thing, which is better than brains." wrote Lord Fisher, one of his admirals.

Unlike Victoria, the king did not meddle with the work of Parliament. But he enjoyed travelling abroad, and tried to make foreign governments more friendly towards Britain. In 1903, he went to Paris. He became the first British monarch to visit the Pope in Rome for 600 years. He was also the first one ever to go to Russia.

At home, Edward enjoyed a hectic social life. He gambled at London clubs and went to horse races at Ascot and Goodwood. He spent much of each winter shooting pheasants in England or grouse in Scotland. He ate huge meals every day. Most wealthy people lived in this very grand manner. To them, Britain seemed a strong and comfortable land, protected by the power of the Empire.

▷ **Edward with a shooting party** on his estate at Sandringham, in Norfolk. He spent more time here than at Buckingham Palace.

◁ **Edward VII welcomes the French fleet** at Portsmouth following the signing in 1904 of an agreement between Britain and France called the *Entente Cordiale*. This ended several long-standing disputes between the two countries. It was a direct result of King Edward's highly popular visit to France in 1903.

▽ **The king (right) with his nephew**, Kaiser Wilhelm II, the Emperor of Germany.

H. M. THE KING AND THE EMPEROR OF GERMANY.

Wealth and wages

Edward often invited rich friends to weekend parties at Sandringham. He might spend more on one dinner than his servants would be paid in a whole year. There was a big difference between the earnings, or salary, of rich and poor.

● The upper classes and wealthy businessmen earned more than £5,000 a year.

● Doctors, lawyers and other professionals earned about £600 a year.

● A farm worker's annual salary was about £30.

● A housemaid in a rich household earned £20 a year, with food and lodging. In the early 1900s a loaf of bread cost about ½ p, a pack of butter 1p and a steak 4p.

At the beginning of Edward VII's reign, there were about 42 million people living in Britain. Only a few of these were rich. In fact 66% of the nation's wealth was in the hands of just 1% of the population. Below them were the middle classes, from doctors and merchants to shopworkers and clerks. Next came the craftsmen and skilled workers. At the bottom was the largest class of all – the ordinary workers and the poor.

In 1901, Seebohm Rowntree made a survey of poor people in York. He found that half of the city's working class lived below the 'poverty line'. This meant that they could not afford enough food and other necessities. Another survey, in 1904, showed that 250,000 people lived in workhouses.

7

VOTES FOR WOMEN

Since the 1880s, women had gained several new rights. They could vote in local elections. There were better chances for them to go to school and to get jobs. But they were still a long way from being equal with men. Women were paid lower wages, and were not allowed to vote in elections for Parliament.

Women's groups had tried to persuade politicians to give them the vote. But the Members of Parliament, or MPs, who were all men, had mostly ignored them. Some even thought that women could not be trusted to make sensible choices, unless guided by men.

In 1903, Emmeline Pankhurst and her daughters founded the Women's Social & Political Union (WSPU). Their aim was to fight more strongly for female 'suffrage' (the right to vote) than ever. The newspapers mocked them, and referred to them as 'suffragettes'.

The motto of the WSPU was *Deeds, not Words*. The Pankhursts organized protest marches and meetings. In 1908 they led a demonstration at the House of Commons. Mrs Pankhurst was sent to prison for refusing to keep the peace.

▷ **Suffragettes smash shop windows in a London street.** Their actions became more violent as they tried to get attention for their cause. Here are some of the things they did:
● chained themselves to railings near the Prime Minister's house in Downing Street, London
● tried to set fire to public buildings and letter boxes
● clashed with police who were guarding Buckingham Palace
● in 1913, Emily Davison died after she threw herself under the king's horse during the Derby race at Epsom.

▽ **Unemployed (out of work) men queueing up for details of jobs** at the Labour Exchange at Camberwell Green in London. These exchanges were set up in 1910 across the country so that men did not need to travel so far to find work.

▽ **In 1906, James Keir Hardie**, the first Labour MP, founded, and became leader of, the Labour Party.

VOTES FOR WOMEN
COME
TO THE
HOUSE O

In spite of the work of the suffragettes, women still did not have the vote by 1914. But when the First World War broke out, they had a new chance to prove their value. As men went to join the armed forces, women took their jobs. Many worked in factories.

After the war, women's importance to the nation was officially recognized by Parliament. Women over 30 years old were allowed to vote in the general election of 1918. At the same time, the voting age for men was lowered to 21. Women were also able to become MPs. The first woman to take her seat in the House of Commons was an American, Nancy Astor. It was not until May 1928 that women over 21 were given the right to vote. Only a month earlier, Emmeline Pankhurst had died.

▽ **A poster attacking the *'Cat & Mouse Act'* of 1913.**
Suffragettes who were sent to jail for their protests and then refused to eat, were at first fed by force. This was unpopular. The Act allowed prisons to release the women and then, when they were better, to re-arrest them.

TREATMENT OF
POLITICAL
PRISONERS
UNDER A
LIBERAL
GOVERNMENT.

GLOOM AND DISASTERS

Edward VII died in 1910 and was succeeded by his son, who became King George V. But now Britain seemed less secure. Already, there was a threat of war in Europe. British politicians and soldiers were worried by the growing strength of Germany.

▷ **Recruits for Lord Kitchener's army in 1914.** Not only had the German navy become a threat to British power at sea, but Germany was anxious to expand its empire, especially in Africa. This often caused conflict with African countries that were part of the British Empire. When war was declared, Lord Kitchener, the War Minister, asked for 500,000 volunteers for the British army.

In the 19th century, the small German states had been united into a single nation by the Prussian chancellor, Bismarck. Under Kaiser (emperor) Wilhelm II, George's cousin, the new Germany used its great industrial power to build a strong navy to rival Britain's.

There were other strong nations in Europe, including Russia, France and the empire of Austria-Hungary. Some made agreements to help each other if they were attacked by an enemy. In 1882, Germany, Austria and Italy formed the Triple Alliance. In 1907, Russia joined Britain and France in the Triple Entente These alliances split Europe into two opposing forces.

▷ **Men at work on a 'Dreadnought' battleship** in Portsmouth dockyard. Another rides at anchor in the harbour. The first of these new ships had been built in only 5 months, and launched in 1906. They each had 10 big guns, and were faster than any other naval ship of the time. Alarmed by this, the Germans started to build similar 'big gun' ships. But these were too big. The Kiel Canal (Germany's only channel to the North Sea) had to be made wider so the battleships could sail out.

△ **Captain R.F. Scott** and his men were beaten in a race to the South Pole by the Norwegian, Amundsen. They died on the journey back in 1912.

△ **The sinking of the liner *Titanic*** was the second great disaster of 1912. Over 1,400 people lost their lives when she hit an iceberg.

As war loomed, Britain hurried to improve its army and navy. A British Expeditionary Force (the BEF) was formed, ready to fight anywhere, and a new fleet of Dreadnoughts was built. Meanwhile, there was growing trouble in Eastern Europe. The Austrians wanted to take control of the Balkan states. In June 1914, the Austrian Archduke Franz Ferdinand was shot dead in Sarajevo by a gunman belonging to a Serbian secret society. A month later, Austro-Hungary declared war on Serbia.

Within a few weeks, Russia and France got ready to fight Austria, and Germany declared war on them both. German troops prepared to invade France. To do so they had to invade Belgium, which was a neutral country (not allied with anyone). Britain had promised to protect the Belgians. So, on 4 August 1914, Britain declared war on Germany. The 'Great War' had begun.

IN THE TRENCHES

The 130,000 soldiers of the BEF landed in France 2 weeks after war was declared. They marched to Belgium to face the German army. Many thought the war would be over by Christmas. But it was to last 4 years, and millions of lives would be lost. The young men of the world were condemned to death.

At first, the German troops forced the French and British to retreat. But in September, at the River Marne, east of Paris, the French stood firm. Then the British and the Belgians drove the Germans back at Ypres, in Flanders. By December, the great German advance had stopped.

A new kind of war now began. Neither side could move forward. Instead, they started to dig systems of trenches to secure their positions. By early 1915, the trenches stretched for over 700 kilometres, from the Belgian coast across France to Switzerland. Life in the trenches was miserable. The soldiers slept in holes dug in the earth. The floors were thick with mud or floodwater, and the air stank of decay and dead bodies. Rats gnawed at the food supplies and clothing. Day and night there was the deafening roar of shells from the artillery.

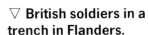

▽ **British soldiers in a trench in Flanders.** Trenches were about 1.5 metres deep with a wall of sandbags at the front for protection from shells. Men had to stay out of sight of enemy snipers.

△ **The Western Front** of the war in early 1915.

▷ **A British soldier**, with his rifle and wearing a gas mask pouch, emerges from a crudely made shelter in a trench in France in 1914.

SINGLE MEN

Hundreds of Thousands of married men have left their homes to fight for **KING & COUNTRY**

SHOW YOUR APPRECIATION

BY FOLLOWING THEIR NOBLE EXAMPLE

◁ **Britain at war.**
Far left: A poster for volunteers to join the army in 1914.
Left centre: Women workers at an aircraft factory.
Left: German airships called Zeppelins dropped bombs on London, killing civilians.

AID POST

The area between the enemy lines was called No Man's Land. In some places, this was less than 30 metres wide. Troops had to run across it when they attacked the enemy, but No Man's Land was usually a sea of mud and shell-holes, blocked with coils of barbed wire. The soldiers made easy targets for the enemy's machine guns.

In spite of this, both sides kept on sending men 'over the top'. On 1 July 1916, Britain and the Allies launched a major attack near the River Somme. On the first day, 20,000 British soldiers were killed. The Battle of the Somme went on for 5 months. The Allies gained only 7 kilometres of ground and lost 600,000 men. The Germans lost just as many.

◁ **The front-line trench** ran along the edge of No Man's Land. Smaller trenches called 'saps' were dug forward towards the enemy lines. They were used for launching attacks or for listening to the enemy. Soldiers spent about a week at a time in the front line before resting.

Breaking the Deadlock

At the end of 1916, the two sides on the Western Front were still stuck in their trenches. In the East, the Russians were being forced back by the Germans and another of their allies, the Turks. In the previous year, British, Australian and New Zealand troops had tried to knock Turkey out of the war but had failed.

▷ **A British tank** rumbles across No Man's Land at Cambrai in France in November 1917. This was the first time tanks were used in large numbers. They were a great success, flattening the barbed wire and armoured against bullets. But many of the tanks broke down or got stuck in trenches, and the troops could not hold the ground they had won.

The big attacks at Gallipoli in Turkey and the Somme were disasters. But this did not stop the Allied commanders from planning more. They believed that one 'Big Push' would quickly end the war.

In April 1917, the French tried to break through the German lines near the Aisne River. The slaughter was so terrible that some French troops mutinied. In June, the British started a 3-month battle for a ridge near Ypres. They took the ridge, but lost 300,000 more men. The following spring, the Germans recaptured the ridge.

There were two more disasters for the Allies in 1917. The Russian Revolution began, and Russia withdrew from the war. And German U-boats started an all-out attack on Allied ships in the Atlantic.

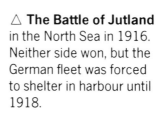

△ **The Battle of Jutland** in the North Sea in 1916. Neither side won, but the German fleet was forced to shelter in harbour until 1918.

▷ **Admirals Lord Jellicoe** (right), Lord Fisher and Lord Beatty led the British fleet.

▷ **A fighter pilot of the Royal Flying Corps.** Aircraft were an important new weapon in the war. At first, they were only used to spy on enemy lines. Soon, the pilots were dropping bombs and shooting at enemy troops and supply depots as well.

△ **A front line British soldier** on the march. He is carrying his heavy pack, rifle, ammunition and a gas mask. After 1915, both sides used poison gas in some attacks.

△ **A sailor of the Royal Navy.** British warships escorted convoys of cargo vessels to protect them against attacks by German surface raiders and 'U-boats' (submarines).

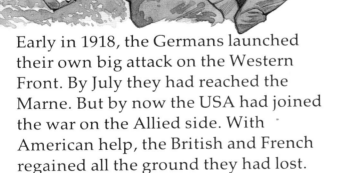

Early in 1918, the Germans launched their own big attack on the Western Front. By July they had reached the Marne. But by now the USA had joined the war on the Allied side. With American help, the British and French regained all the ground they had lost.

The Germans realized that they could not win. Turkey and Austria had already been defeated. The British navy had blocked German ports, so that food supplies could not get in. Many German people were starving. On 11 November 1918, the Germans surrendered.

The war had damaged Britain much less than her European allies. Yet 750,000 British soldiers had died, and over 1,500,000 had been badly wounded.

△ **Douglas Haig**, who became commander of the British Army in 1915. He planned the tragic 'Big Push' of 1917.

▷ **A graveyard filled with the war dead** in Poperinghe, France. Altogether, more than 10 million soldiers and civilians died in the war.

FIGHTING FOR HOME RULE

Irish people had been demanding Home Rule for their country since the 1870s. They wanted to stay a part of Britain but have their own parliament. In 1914, the British government at last agreed to Home Rule. But it was delayed by the start of the First World War.

There was another problem: religion. Most of the Irish were Catholics. But Ulster, in the north, was a mainly Protestant area. The Protestants feared that Home Rule would allow the Catholics to take control of all Ireland. They formed their own army, called the Ulster Volunteer Force.

Meanwhile, some Irish Catholics were not happy with Home Rule either. They wanted Ireland to break free of Britain and become a republic (have no monarch). These people were known as Republicans. Led by Patrick Pearse, the Republicans rose in revolt on Easter Monday 1916. They seized the General Post Office in Dublin and formed their own government. Within a few days, British troops had forced them to surrender. Fourteen of the ringleaders were executed. Their deaths caused great anger against the British in Ireland.

△ **A march by supporters of Sinn Fein**, the Irish Republican party. Sinn Fein (meaning 'Ourselves Alone') had been founded in 1905. Its first leader, Arthur Griffith, helped to organize the Easter Rising in Dublin. Sinn Fein is still a strong political party in Ireland today.

▷ **Members of the Ulster Volunteer Force carry guns ashore** at Larne, County Antrim, in April 1914. The 25,000 German rifles had been brought by a cargo ship at night. The Protestants of Ulster were arming themselves to fight against Home Rule. The Republicans in the South were also buying guns. In 1915, one of their leaders, Roger Casement, went to Germany for help. It sent a ship full of guns, but this was caught by a British patrol boat. Casement was hanged for treason.

⊲ **British troops at a barricade** in Talbot Street, Dublin, during the Easter Rising of 1916. The British brought in heavy artillery to shell rebel strongholds in the city centre. Over 450 people died and 3,000 were wounded in the rebellion.

▷ **How Ireland was divided in 1921.** The six counties of Northern Ireland stayed part of the United Kingdom.

▷ **William Butler Yeats** was an Irish poet and playwright. He wrote several poems about the Irish fight for liberty. In 1904, he helped found Dublin's Abbey Theatre.

At the end of the war, the republicans took up their struggle again. Sinn Fein members of the British House of Commons formed their own parliament in Dublin in 1919. At the same time, Michael Collins founded the Irish Republican Army (the IRA), which attacked policemen, soldiers, military bases and government buildings. In 1921, the British government made a treaty with the rebels. Ireland was divided into two parts. The six Protestant counties in Ulster became Northern Ireland, part of the United Kingdom. The rest became the Irish Free State, which governed itself but stayed under British rule.

But this did not end the troubles. The Republicans fought on to try to win complete freedom from Britain. Nearly 4,000 people were killed before the civil war stopped in 1923.

HOUSES AND HOMES

After the First World War, the Prime Minister of the time, David Lloyd George, promised to make Britain "a fit country for heroes to live in". He built council houses in place of the old slums. By 1939, there were nearly a million new council homes. They were let to tenants at a rent of about 10 shillings (50p) a week.

Meanwhile, private houses were being built even more quickly. About three million were constructed in the 1920s and 1930s. Many of them were semi-detached (two houses joined together). These were cheaper to build than single (detached) houses. They were also cheaper to buy. For the first time, many middle-class people could buy their own house by taking out a loan from a bank called a mortgage.

A large number of these 'semis' were built on the edges of towns. They created pleasant new suburbs, within easy reach of the countryside. But they were also near enough to the city centres for residents to go to work by bus or train. In this way, towns began to spread rapidly outwards, especially along major roads. Whole new communities grew up, such as Harrow near London. They had their own shops and cinemas.

▷ **A semi-detached home in the 1930s suburbs.** Like many other 'semis', it has been built in a mock-Tudor style, with weather-proofed timber beams and diamond-shaped 'leaded' window panes. The bricks on the upper storey are covered with concrete. Upstairs there are two bedrooms and a small 'box' room, as well as a bathroom. All new houses now had running water and inside lavatories. Downstairs are two living rooms, a hall and a kitchen. The kitchen is quite small. It contains only a cooker, a sink and a tub for washing clothes. There is a small garden at the front, and a bigger one behind. A house like this cost about £600 to buy.

△ **The Hoover factory** at Perivale, West London. This was one of many grand new factories built in the 1920s and 1930s. They were often built with other factories on industrial estates. Many produced household goods, such as canned food, vacuum cleaners and cookers.

▷ **This household has no servants.** New machines, or 'modern conveniences', now help with most of the housework. The floors are cleaned with a vacuum cleaner, powered by electricity. The lights are also electric. By 1938, nearly two-thirds of all homes were wired for electricity from the new National Grid. The cooker is heated by gas, but the fire in the sitting room still burns coal. Wives ran the home. Few wives went out to work.

△ **Many families now owned a car**, so new houses were often built with a drive and a garage. This car is an Austin, a popular make of the 1930s.

19

LEISURE AND PASTIMES

Although the people of Europe had problems rebuilding their lives after the First World War ended, by the 1920s and 1930s things were looking better. More British people had more money and spare time to enjoy themselves than ever before.

△ **Holidaymakers off for an outing in 1925.** They are riding in an early kind of motor coach called a charabanc. It had solid rubber tyres and no roof, and was probably very uncomfortable.

▷ **Crowds and newspaper seller outside a London cinema** in the early 1930s.

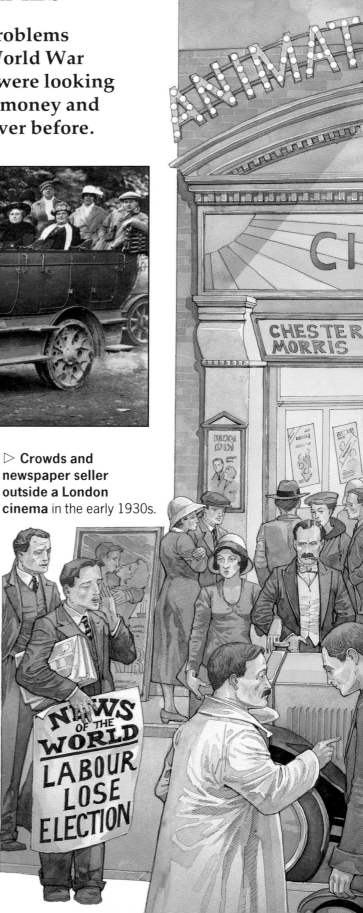

There were many new kinds of entertainment. The most popular was the cinema. Silent films had been drawing huge crowds since before the war. In 1927 the first 'talkies', or sound films, appeared. Most films were made in the USA. They showed a glamorous world that was very different from the way most British people lived.

By the 1930s, nearly half the adult population was going to the cinema at least once a week. These 'picture houses' were not only cheap, but warmer than most people's homes.

There were new styles of music to listen to, and dancing quickly became a craze. American jazz was first heard in Britain in 1919. It was soon played by bands in hotels and dance halls. The first Palais de Danse (Dance Palace) opened in Hammersmith, London, in 1919, and was soon copied in other cities. Music could also be heard at home, on gramophones and radios. The first modern gramophone had appeared in 1905, and by the 1920s many households had one. In 1922, the British Broadcasting Company (later Corporation – the BBC) was formed. It began to transmit regular radio programmes of news, talks and music. 'Listening in' soon grew into the most popular kind of entertainment at home. In 1936, the BBC started the world's first television service, which was broadcast from London.

In the new age of cheap entertainment, religion became a less powerful part of daily life. Fewer people went to church and chapel services. This was partly due to the war. The horrors of the trenches had destroyed the religious faith of many soldiers and their families.

△ **The Radio Times** for Christmas 1925. Owners of radios had to pay a licence fee of 10 shillings (50p) each year. In 1925, there were over 1.6 million licences issued. By 1939, the total had shot up to 9 million. Through radio, ordinary people were able to hear about world events, even in remote areas.

◁ **Football fans at the West Ham versus Arsenal F.A. Cup tie in 1930.** The final was played at Wembley Stadium. The other old established sports, such as cricket, tennis and horse racing, grew even more popular. And many new sports began, like speedway and greyhound racing. They were popular with working class people.

TRANSPORT IN THE '20s AND '30s

In 1909, an aircraft had flown across the English Channel for the first time. Only 10 years later, there were regular passenger flights between London and Paris. Aircraft were made bigger and faster, and flew greater distances. In 1919, two English pilots, Alcock and Brown, were the first to fly across the Atlantic.

By the late 1920s, passengers could travel by air to many parts of the world. Britain's Imperial Airways flew to India, Africa and the Far East. The aircraft were slow (their top speed was less than 160 km/h) but very comfortable. They were also very safe: not one passenger was ever lost.

British pilots went on finding new air routes, primarily to carry mail. In 1926, Alan Cobham captained the first aircraft to fly to Australia and back. In 1930, Amy Johnson became the first to fly solo (alone) to Australia. But also in 1930 the airship R101 crashed in France. This put an end to hopes that airships (lifted by gas) would be the airliners of the future.

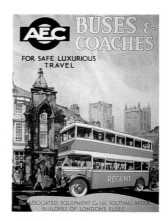

△ **A 1930s bus poster.**

▽ **Airline passengers** at London's first major airport at Croydon.

22

Air travel was only for the rich. So was travel by ocean liner. The big passenger ships, such as the *Mauretania* and the *Queen Mary*, were like floating hotels. Their main route was across the Atlantic, between Liverpool and New York.

There was more opportunity for ordinary people to travel, too, even if they could not afford to go abroad. Trains were still very popular and cheap. The railways also became much more efficient in the 1920s.

But trains now had new rivals – the motor car and the lorry. New factories could make vehicles quickly on their 'assembly lines'. And the price of cars actually fell, from an average of £260 in 1924, to only £130 in 1935. This meant that many more people, including ordinary workers, could afford to buy a car. By 1930, there were well over a million cars on the roads in Britain.

Better roads were needed to cope with the rise in traffic. They were covered with tarmac (stones bound with tar) and lined with white paint. Towns soon became noisier and more dangerous.

▷ **Sir Malcolm Campbell** and his streamlined car *Bluebird*. Campbell broke many land speed records. In 1935 he was the first to reach 485 km/h.

△ **Trains, railway passengers and porters** at Paddington Station in London in the 1930s. But by this time, many more people were travelling by bus and coach. These had lower fares than trains, and could reach places where there were no railways.

◁ **Two more British record-breakers.** The luxury liner *Queen Mary* made the fastest crossing of the Atlantic in 1936, taking just 3 days and 20 hours. The *Mallard* became the fastest-ever steam locomotive in 1938, when it reached a speed of 201 km/h.

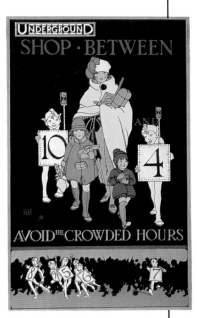

△ **A 1920s poster** encouraging shoppers in London not to travel during the 'rush-hours'.

OLD INDUSTRIES IN DECLINE

From about 1925, the economy of the United States declined. This caused problems in Britain. In October 1926, there was a collapse of the New York Financial Market (the Wall Street Crash). Britain's exports fell from £840 million in 1929 to £460 million in 1931.

▷ **Out of work miners** in a South Wales industrial town in the 1930s. They are picking over a waste heap from a mine to look for coal to heat their homes.

▷ **A volunteer drives a bus during the 1926 General Strike.** The policeman is there to protect him from any action by strikers (although in fact the strike was mostly peaceful). Thousands of volunteers helped to keep important services and supplies going while the real workers stayed away. They drove buses and trains, sorted mail, and delivered food and other essential goods. Soldiers also did these jobs.

Coal, with steel, textiles and ships, had been Britain's most important products for nearly 200 years. But now these old, heavy industries were in decline. Coal and steel could be produced more cheaply in the USA, Germany and other countries. Cheaper cotton cloth was being made in India and the Far East. Fewer people wanted to buy from Britain.

In 1926, coal miners asked the Trades Union Congress (TUC) for help in its struggle with the mine owners. The owners were to reduce miners' wages and increase their hours of work. On 4 May the TUC called for a General Strike. Railwaymen, factory workers, printers, builders, bus drivers and many others did not go to work. Much of industry and transport came to a halt. But, only 9 days later, the TUC told workers to end the strike. It realized that they could not win. The miners stayed on strike until August. Many were by then very poor and starving. In the end, they had to accept lower wages and longer hours.

◁ **Oswald Mosley** (on the right), leader of the British Union of Fascists, a political party based on the ideas of Adolf Hitler's Nazis in Germany. Mosley used the Nazi flag, shown below. The Fascists blamed the country's economic problems on foreigners. They held violent meetings in poor areas of London.

The growth in industry in Asia and the Far East caused a decline in wealth in many European countries and the USA. We now call it the Great Depression. In Britain, it meant that many factories, mines and shipyards had to be closed down, and people thrown out of work.

By early 1931, there were over three million unemployed workers. Jobless people had only the government's 'dole' money to live on. In 1931, the dole for a married couple was £1 7s 6d (£1.37) a week. Anybody who claimed unemployment pay had to pass a 'means test' to make sure that they were not earning any extra money. If they were, this was deducted from their dole.

One of the worst hit areas was Jarrow, in north-east England. In 1936, 200 men marched from Jarrow to London to ask for help from Parliament. The Prime Minister refused to see them.

THE SECOND WORLD WAR

By the late 1930s, Europe was sliding towards another war. Germany was ruled by Adolf Hitler and his Nazis. Hitler wanted Germany to be powerful again. He built up a strong army and air force, and began to bully and invade weak countries nearby.

▷ **Pilots of the Royal Air Force** (RAF) race to their Spitfires to fight off an attack by German bombers. After the fall of France, Hitler planned to invade Britain across the Channel. First, he had to defeat the RAF. In July 1940 the Battle of Britain began for control of the sky. The Germans tried to bomb ships, towns and airfields. But RAF fighters drove them back. Hitler gave up his invasion plan.

In September 1939, the Germans invaded Poland. Britain and France quickly declared war on Germany. In the spring of 1940, Hitler's army swept through north-west Europe. Denmark, Norway, the Netherlands and Belgium fell to the Germans in a few weeks.

The British Army was trapped at Dunkirk, on the French coast. Hundreds of ships, from naval destroyers to tiny fishing boats, crossed the Channel to rescue them. While the Germans attacked, over 330,000 Allied soldiers were ferried to England.

The German tanks and troops rolled on into France. Then Italy joined the war on the side of the Germans. In June 1940, the French were forced to surrender.

△ **Newspaper posters announce the German invasion** of Poland on 1 September 1939. Hitler had agreed not to go to war with Russia, and to share Poland in return.

How Europe fell to the Germans:
1936 Hitler takes over the Rhineland, a neutral area of Germany.
1938 German troops unite Austria with Germany and seize part of Czechoslovakia.
1939 Germans complete their invasion of Czechoslovakia, then march into Poland.
1940 Germany invades Denmark and Norway (April), Belgium and the Netherlands (May), and France (June). Britain and its empire now stands alone against Germany and Italy. Other countries in Europe remain neutral.

◁ **Adolf Hitler** (far left) had become leader of Germany in 1934. He believed that Britain would be eager to make peace after France had surrendered. Winston Churchill (left) became the British Prime Minister in May 1940. He stirred the people with his strong faith in victory.

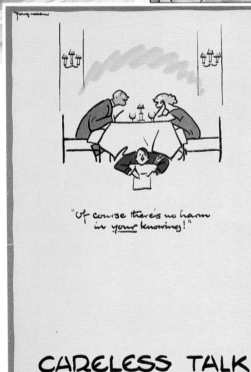

"Of course there's no harm in *your* knowing!"

CARELESS TALK COSTS LIVES

△ **A British cartoon poster of 1940.** It warns people not to give information to German spies by mistake.

By early 1941, things looked very bleak for Britain. Nearly all her allies had been defeated, and she was now almost alone in Europe. That spring, the Germans conquered Yugoslavia and Greece. They also captured the important island of Crete. In North Africa, German tank units led by Erwin Rommel drove the British out of Libya and deep into Egypt.

It was even more desperate at sea. German U-boats prowled the Atlantic Ocean, hunting cargo ships bound for Britain. Each month, they sank many ships with their torpedoes. This meant that the British went short of food and other vital supplies such as petrol.

But in June 1941, Hitler made his biggest mistake. When the RAF won the Battle of Britain, he gave up his invasion plan. Then he turned east and attacked Russia, once Germany's partner.

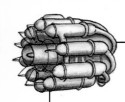

THE HOME FRONT

"Hitler knows that he will have to break us in this island or lose the war. If we can stand up to him, all Europe may be free." Churchill spoke these words on BBC radio in June 1940. He was warning the British people that there was great hardship to come.

The Second World War changed everyone's life in Britain. It was not only the fighting forces who were in danger. Night after night, German aircraft dropped bombs on London and other towns. In 1944, there were also 'flying bombs' and rockets. These weapons destroyed public buildings, factories, roads, railways and homes. More than 60,000 people were killed in Britain during what was called 'the Blitz'.

Many families built air-raid shelters in their gardens. Others went to public shelters. In London, people slept in the Underground railway stations. Many city children were evacuated (sent away) to spend the war in the safety of families living in the countryside.

The government asked people at home to help with the war effort. As so many young men were fighting overseas, most jobs had to be done by women or older people. 'Land girls' and school children helped on farms. Men joined the part-time army called the Home Guard, or spent the nights watching for fires caused by air raids. People also got ready to fight a German invasion. Road signs were removed. Beaches were covered with barbed wire. Flat fields were littered with old cars and lorries to stop enemy aircraft from landing.

▷ **Volunteers clear up after an air raid.** Rubble was moved away and dangerous ruins made safe. The wounded were taken to hospital. People who had lost their homes were found rooms in other houses. They were fed by mobile canteens. Apart from London, the worst-hit cities were Coventry, Liverpool, Birmingham and Bristol.

△ **Parts for air-raid shelters** are delivered to residents in Islington, London, in 1939. The shelters were made from corrugated (crinkled) sheets of iron bolted together. Most people learned to "live with the bombs", but some city-dwellers fled to the countryside each night, pushing their possessions in carts and prams.

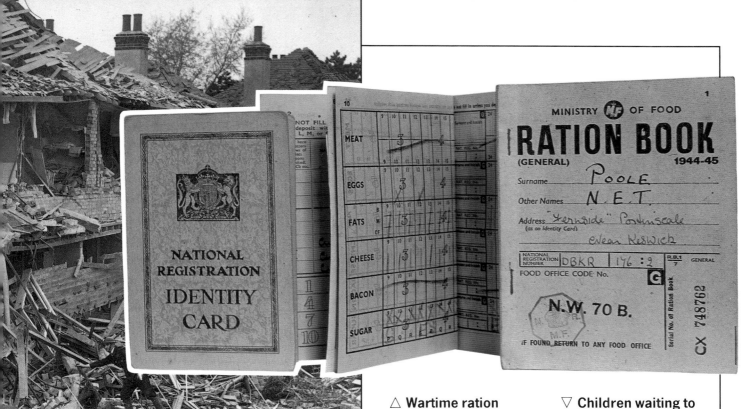

MINISTRY OF FOOD

RATION BOOK
(GENERAL) 1944-45

Surname POOLE

Other Names N.E.T.

Address "Fernside" Portinscale
(as on Identity Card)
Near Keswick

NATIONAL REGISTRATION NUMBER DBKR 176:9

FOOD OFFICE CODE No.

N.W. 70 B.

IF FOUND RETURN TO ANY FOOD OFFICE

CX 748762

NATIONAL REGISTRATION IDENTITY CARD

△ **Wartime ration books and an identity card.** Clothes, coal and petrol were rationed as well as food. Each book contained coupons which were torn out when goods were purchased. After 1939, everyone had to carry identity cards to prove who they were.

▽ **Children waiting to be evacuated by train** from their home town. They carry small bundles of luggage. Around their necks are labels to show where they are going. Many town children had never been to the countryside before. They were frightened.

As the war went on, supplies of many goods ran short. Food was rationed, so that everyone had a fair share. Each person was allowed only small portions of meat, butter and eggs. Gardeners 'dug for victory' by growing extra vegetables on parks and other spare land.

Nothing was wasted. Old clothes were patched or turned into curtains or rugs. Firewood was gathered from beaches and bomb sites. Iron railings, old saucepans and any sort of scrap metal were collected to make ships and tanks. Housewives, office girls and older schoolchildren knitted thousands of socks and scarves for troops overseas.

Winning the War 1942-45

The tide of war began to turn during 1942. In 1941, Hitler's troops had just failed to seize Moscow, and then winter arrived. Thousands of German soldiers starved or were frozen to death. In North Africa, the Germans were defeated by troops from the British Empire under General Montgomery at El Alamein.

◁ **American GIs** (soldiers) having fun in Britain. (GI is short for General Issue, a term for ordinary military clothing.) When the USA entered the war, many thousands of GIs came to Britain. Some were on their way to fight in Europe, others to get ready for the D-Day invasion. A force of 3,000 US troops helped clear and rebuild bombed houses in London. The GIs cheered the British with their cigarettes, music and chocolate bars.

Meanwhile, Britain had a new ally – and a new enemy. At the end of 1941, Japan had attacked the US Navy at Pearl Harbor, in Hawaii. The Americans, and then the British, had declared war on the Japanese. The war now stretched round the world.

At first, Japan had great success. Japanese troops conquered most of South-east Asia, including Singapore and Burma. By the end of 1942, they threatened India. But soon they were attacked on both sides. From the west, British and Empire forces began to regain Burma. From the east, US troops advanced through the Pacific islands and bombed Japan itself.

The Americans also helped the British to drive the Germans out of North Africa. In July 1943, the Allies invaded Italy. The Italians quickly surrendered, but the Germans fought on. At the same time, the US Air Force joined the RAF in a series of massive bombing raids on German cities.

◁ **British tanks** drive forward across the desert at the Battle of El Alamein in 1942. The Allies broke through the German lines, and forced them to retreat over 2,200 kilometres into Tunisia. It was a turning point. The Germans in North Africa surrendered in May 1943.

How Europe was freed from the Germans:
1943 February – Germans suffer huge defeat at Stalingrad, in Russia. September – Allies invade Italy from the South.
1944 June – Allies land in Northern France. August – Paris recaptured by Allies.
1945 February – Allies cross German border. May – German surrender.

Area under Hitler's control 1942

BRITAIN
RUSS
Moscow
Staling
Berlin
GERMANY
Normandy
FRANCE
El Alamein

◁ **British troops landing on a Normandy beach on D-Day.** In the background are the landing craft which carried them over from southern England.

The Allied commanders now planned a return to France. Troops in Britain trained for D-Day. On 6 June 1944, a fleet of boats carried an invasion army to the beaches of Normandy. Other troops were landed by glider or parachute.

Within a few weeks, France and Belgium had been recaptured. The Allies marched on into Germany in early 1945. From the east came the Russian soldiers, who had driven the Nazis from Russia and eastern Europe. Berlin fell in April, and Hitler killed himself. Germany surrendered on 7 May. There were huge celebrations throughout Europe.

◁ **The first atomic bomb**, dropped by the US Air Force on Hiroshima in Japan on 6 August 1945, killing 100,000 people. After a second bomb was dropped on Nagasaki, the Japanese surrendered on 2 September 1945.

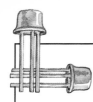

REBUILDING BRITAIN

"Poverty is one only of five giants on the road of reconstruction. The others are Disease, Ignorance, Squalor and Idleness." An economist wrote this in a report on social problems in 1942. The Labour Party came to power in 1945, and tried to beat these giants.

After the war, the British people showed that they wanted a change in society. They voted for a Labour government instead of Churchill and the Conservatives. Labour, led by Clement Attlee, promised to set up a new 'Welfare State'.

The first problem was money. The British government had spent so much on the war that it owed £3,000 million to other countries. Roads, docks, factories and houses lay in ruins.

Attlee and his ministers borrowed another £900 million from the USA. This was used to buy new machines and build new factories. New industries, such as chemicals, car-making and electrical goods, were set up. Many older industries were nationalized (controlled by the government). These included electricity, the railways, coal and shipbuilding.

◁ **Children enjoy the end of sweet rationing in April 1949.** Sweets had been rationed since 1940. Even after the war, many goods remained in short supply and were rationed. Coal and other heating fuel was scarce. This caused much hardship, especially during the bitterly cold winter of 1946-47.

▷ **Visitors to the Festival of Britain in 1951.** This exhibition of modern inventions, buildings and designs, plus a funfair, was held on London's South Bank as "a tonic to the nation".

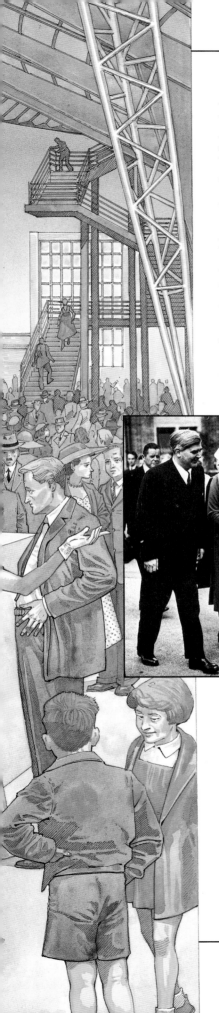

Attlee's government was in power until 1951. It set up a welfare system in which the state could help everyone, rich or poor. It also gave women many more rights, especially if they were married or widowed (their husband had died). In 1946 the first family allowances were paid. Mothers could collect 5 shillings (25p) a week for each child except the eldest. In 1948, a new National Insurance scheme started. Workers paid money to the scheme each week. In return, the government gave them benefits (money) when they were ill, unemployed or stopped from working in some other way. The very poor could also claim an extra payment called National Assistance.

The National Health Service was founded in the same year. This provided free health care for all. People no longer had to pay for treatment by doctors and dentists, for medicines, or for spectacles. The Ministry of Health took charge of hospitals.

△ **Aneurin Bevan**, the Minister of Health, visits a hospital on the first day of the new National Health Service (NHS) in 1948. Many doctors did not want to join the NHS because they would not earn so much money. To solve the problem, Bevan allowed them to treat private patients as well as NHS ones.

△ **New council houses being built.** Because of wartime bombing, there was a shortage of houses. By 1951, 800,000 new council homes had been built. Many people were also living in temporary 'prefabs', which were one-storey huts made of wood and metal. New towns were also begun, such as Stevenage.

△ **A domestic science class** in 1952. A new system of schools had been planned by the government in 1944. This was to provide free education for all children of secondary age. Those who passed an exam at 11 years old would go to grammar schools. Others went to secondary modern schools.

END OF THE EMPIRE

At midnight on 15 August 1947, India became an independent state. After over 160 years of British rule, the Indians now governed themselves. The British Empire had begun to break up. Weakened by the war, Britain could no longer afford to keep all its distant colonies. Many of them wanted independence.

Several larger countries, including South Africa, Australia, Ireland and Canada, had ruled themselves since 1931. They were the first members of what was called the Commonwealth of Nations. This was a group of countries which had once been part of the Empire.

Burma and Ceylon (Sri Lanka) were given their independence soon after India. During the 1950s, they were followed by such countries as Brunei, Malaysia, Ghana, Kenya and Sudan.

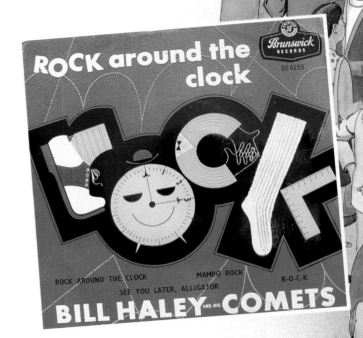

△ **Cover (sleeve) for a 'rock and roll' pop music record** released in Britain around 1958.

◁ **Queen Elizabeth II** and her husband, Prince Philip, on a visit to the Gambia in 1961. The queen had come to the throne in 1952. She had been crowned in a grand ceremony at Westminster Abbey in 1953. The queen has toured every nation in the Commonwealth at least once.

△ **West Indians in London in 1956.** About 125,000 people from the Caribbean came to live in Britain between 1948 and 1958. They hoped to escape the poverty in their own country. Immigrants also came from other parts of the Commonwealth, such as India, Pakistan and West Africa.

▷ **Watching television** grew into the most popular kind of home entertainment. Far right: Some of the 3,000 people who marched from London to Aldermaston in Berkshire to protest against nuclear research in 1958. After this, the march for the Campaign for Nuclear Disarmament (CND) took place every year.

◁ **Teenagers spent much of their leisure time together.** With different interests from their parents, they felt a distinct 'generation gap'.

Britain also changed rapidly during the 1950s. The standard of living rose. People were healthier and better educated than ever before, thanks largely to the welfare state. Many were also richer. Young people, in particular, had more money to spend. For the first time, clothes, music and fashion products were made just for them.

In 1955 the first 'teddy boys' appeared. They wore tight trousers, long jackets and pointed shoes. Their hero was the American singer Elvis Presley. Rock and roll music hit Britain from America in 1957, when Bill Haley and his group toured the country. Older people hated the new music.

GOOD TIMES: THE 1960s

"You've never had it so good", said Prime Minister Harold Macmillan in 1959. He meant that the British were living more comfortably than at any other time in their history. The grim years of rationing were over. By the early 1960s, most people had cosier homes, higher wages and more leisure time than ever.

The pace of change got faster. Cities changed, as tower blocks of flats were built. The countryside changed, as motorways cut across the landscape. Capital punishment (hanging) was abolished as a penalty for murder. The contraceptive pill allowed women to choose when to have a baby.

▽ **Over 250,000 people** went to the Rolling Stones open-air pop concert in London's Hyde Park.

△ **Some of the clothes and hair styles worn by young people in the 1960s.** For the first time, bright new fashions were made especially for teenagers.

▷ **An early comprehensive school.** At 'comprehensives', 11- to 18-year-olds of different abilities were taught together.

In some ways, 1960s Britain seemed to be leading the world. The Beatles from Liverpool were the most successful pop group ever. The England football team won the 1966 World Cup. 'Swinging London' was the centre of fashion.

Young people began to make themselves heard. The long hair of the boys, and the short skirts of the girls, shocked many adults. Students held protest meetings about conditions at new universities. Gangs of working-class youngsters, called 'mods' and 'rockers', held fights at the seaside.

Many old-fashioned values were questioned. Satire programmes, such as the BBC's *That Was the Week That Was*, mocked politicians. Actors in the musical *Hair* took off their clothes on stage. Some people demanded that the drug marijuana should be made legal.

△ **Bobby Moore, the England captain**, holds the World Cup football trophy aloft. England won the 1966 final at Wembley.

△ **Pop music** was heard everywhere, on portable, transistor radios ('trannies') or on stereo record players.

British scientists also brought changes. The hovercraft began services to France in 1966. The Austin Mini was the best-selling small car. The aircraft Concorde, built with French help, was the first passenger plane to fly faster than sound. And nuclear power stations were built.

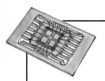

TROUBLES AND STRIKES

The 1970s were a time of great unrest in Britain. Trouble flared up again between Catholics and Protestants in Northern Ireland. Scots and Welsh nationalists sought home rule. Trade unionists demanded higher wages as prices rose sharply.

Women were also campaigning for better treatment. In 1975, two new laws gave women a greater chance of equality at work. The Equal Pay Act meant that women should not be paid less than men for doing the same job. The Sex Discrimination Act stopped employers from refusing women jobs simply because they were women.

By 1980, over one-third of the workforce was female – more than ever before. This caused changes in many people's lives. Wives wanted to spend less time shopping or cooking at home. They began to buy most of their food in convenient supermarkets instead of traditional grocery shops or markets. Or they bought ready cooked meals at the growing number of 'fast-food' shops.

▷ **A family checks in** at an airport for a foreign holiday. Cheap 'package' trips abroad became very popular, especially to Spain and Greece. The number of air passengers doubled during the 1970s, reaching over 40 million a year. In 1977, Freddie Laker launched his Skytrain flights to New York. Tickets cost only £59 each way – far less than other companies.

▷ **An Asian shopkeeper.** Many Asian immigrants opened grocery and newspaper shops. They were willing to stay open for long hours. By 1978, over 1.9 million people from Commonwealth countries had settled in Britain. But by then new limits had stopped all new immigrants except for relations of those already settled in Britain.

▷ **Factory workers strike over low pay** in 1977. Factories like this one closed down as British industry declined. Reasons for this included:
● **Productivity** British workers took longer to produce goods than in other countries. This made the goods more expensive.
● **Cheap imports** In 1973, Britain joined the EEC (European Economic Community, or Common Market). Goods from EEC countries did not have high import taxes.
● **Oil prices** In 1973, the price of oil (used for fuel) from the Middle East rose sharply.

△ **1970s fashions.** Women and men wore trousers which were flared (wide) at the bottom, and platform shoes, which had very thick soles. Most young men had long hair.

The biggest problem for governments of the 1970s was the struggle with the trade unions. The unions had grown very strong, and often took strike action to fight for higher wages and better conditions. In 1970, there were 4,000 strikes.

The Conservative government, led by Edward Heath, tried to bring the unions under control. In 1972, the miners asked their employers for a huge pay rise. The government would not allow it to be paid. So the miners went on an all-out strike. Power stations ran out of coal, and the electricity supply to homes, offices, and schools had to be turned off for long periods. A 3-day working week was introduced.

When the Labour Party came to power again in 1974, they faced the same trouble. Labour put a limit on the size of wage increases. Many big unions came out on strike to protest. Car workers, lorry drivers, dustmen and many others took action during the 1979 'winter of discontent'.

◁ **An Irish rioter** throws a petrol bomb at British soldiers and police in Belfast in 1972.

The Irish Problem
Northern Ireland was again a scene of violence:
1969 Northern Irish Catholics riot, angry at the bad treatment from Protestants. British troops are sent to stop the riots.
1970 The Provisional IRA begins a terrorist war against British troops and Protestants.
1972 On 30 January, 'Bloody Sunday', 13 rioters are shot dead in Derry by British soldiers.
1974 An IRA bomb kills 17 people in Birmingham.
1976 Women in Belfast campaign for peace.
1979 Earl Mountbatten, a cousin of the queen, and MP Airey Neave are both killed by IRA bombs.

THE 1980S AND INTO THE '90S

In 1979, the Conservative Party was voted into power again. Margaret Thatcher became the first woman Prime Minister. She soon passed new laws to control the trade unions. She also took away some controls on industry to help it grow. She raised money for the government by selling state-owned businesses.

Thatcher was respected as a tough leader. One foreign president called her "the Iron Lady". But her policies were disliked by many people. They felt she was encouraging selfishness and making the gap between rich and poor wider.

Certainly Britain became richer during the mid-1980s. Some new industries, such as electronics and financial services, grew rapidly. More people than ever owned their own homes. Oil from the North Sea made fuel prices cheaper.

But this 'boom' soon ended. British industry faced increasing competition from abroad, and the country imported more goods than ever before. Many factories, coal mines and steelworks closed down. Over three million people were unemployed by the early 1990s.

There were also growing worries about the environment. For years, air, water and soil had been polluted by waste matter, mostly from factories, quarries and farms. In 1991, one in four British beaches was found to be too dirty to use and many rivers were polluted.

At the same time, large areas of the countryside were disappearing under new roads and housing estates. And some modern farming methods were threatening British wildlife.

△ **A 1982 cartoon.** Britain was at war with Argentina in the Falkland Islands. The inhabitants of the islands wanted to remain under British rule. Thatcher's Britain was victorious, but it was a costly war.

▷ **An aerial view of Canary Wharf tower complex being built in the late 1980s.** This new development in London's former docklands was expected to boost commerce and local businesses. It has not, and many of the buildings are still unoccupied.

▷ **Firemen fight to put out a burning car** during riots in Tottenham, London, in October 1985. The riot was sparked off by anger at police treatment of black people in the area. In scenes of great violence, a white policeman was hacked to death by the crowd. Four more policemen were wounded by gunshots and more than 200 others were injured.

Cummings

E.E.C.

"Hope he won't break the machine before we break him in..."

△ **In 1990, some EEC leaders** thought that Britain was too slow in making decisions. Here, President Mitterrand of France (left) and Chancellor Kohl of Germany (right) try to force Prime Minister John Major to agree to their conditions. In 1986, Mitterrand had signed an agreement with Margaret Thatcher to build the Channel Tunnel between France and England. But while the French pressed ahead with constructing road and high-speed rail links to the tunnel, Britain has been slow to act.

A Century of Change

We have already highlighted many of the ways in which Britain changed during the 20th century. The figures on these pages show some other changes. They are to do with the population. There are now 20 million more Britons than there were in 1901. They are richer and healthier – and they live much longer.

This means that there are more old people than ever before. At the start of the century, about 4% of the population was over 65 years old. Today, that figure is about 13%. At the same time, there are fewer children being born.

So families have got smaller. In 1901, there were 4.6 people in an average household. Today, there are only 2.5. This is partly because there are many more families with a single parent. It is also due to the fall in the number of servants. In 1861, about 14% of households had at least one servant who lived with the family. By 1951, the figure was about 1%. Today, very few households have any servants at all.

Another major change has taken place at work. At the start of the century, nearly three-quarters of working people worked with their hands (manually), actually making things. Today, most people work in shops and offices.

Since 1945, the large numbers of immigrants from Commonwealth countries have also brought changes. One of the biggest is in religion. Non-Christian religions, such as Islam and Sikhism, have grown rapidly, while the Christian Church of England and other Protestant churches have shrunk.

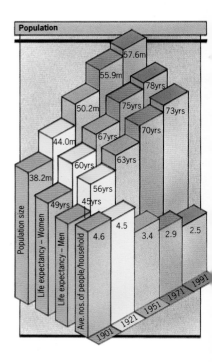

▷ **Life and families.**
In the first part of the century, the population grew fast. Since the 1970s, this growth has slowed down. Fewer babies are being born. But people born today can expect to live much longer than those born in 1901. Women, as always, can expect to live longer than men.

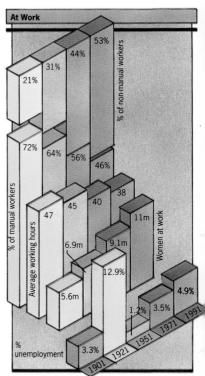

▷ **At work.**
There have been several major changes in work in Britain. The number of working women has doubled during the century. The number of unemployed people has risen even faster, especially since 1945. (The pre-war totals for unemployment were not gathered in the same way, so should not be compared exactly.) People also spend less time at work each week – if they can find a job to start with!

The graphs on these pages show some of the ways in which life in Britain has changed during the 20th century. The figures come from the national survey called the census. This is made every 10 years. (The details have been somewhat simplified.)

▽ Spending
During the century, people have been able to spend more money on 'consumer' goods. At the same time, they have spent less on food.

▽ The 12 countries of the European Community
(the EC, formerly the EEC). Its aim is to make trade in Europe cheaper and stronger. EC countries have united to sell their goods abroad. The Community now contains more people and produces more goods than the USA.

How Britain joined the European Community:
1957 The Community is founded. Britain decides not to join.
1963 Britain now tries to join but is rejected by France.
1973 Britain at last becomes a member of the Community. Britons are elected to serve in the European Parliament. Ireland also joins the EEC.
1993 The Treaty of Maastricht brings freer trade between member states. Britain refuses to agree to the whole treaty.

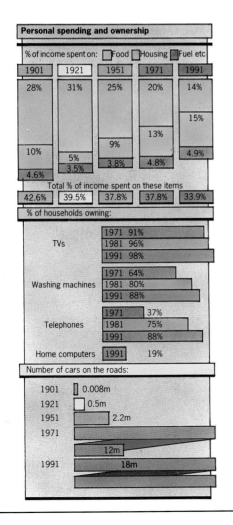

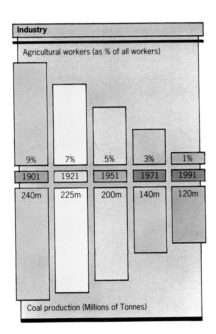

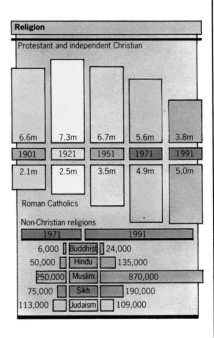

△ **Industry, mining and agriculture.** The amount of coal mined in Britain has fallen sharply partly because there are other new kinds of fuel such as nuclear power. Farming is now a rich industry, machines having replaced people.

△ **Religion.** While the population has grown, the number of members of Christian churches has fallen. Protestant churches especially have lost support. The arrival of many Asian immigrants has caused growth in non-Christian religions.

FAMOUS PEOPLE OF MODERN TIMES

The Beatles, formed in 1959, were the most successful rock group in history. The members were John Lennon, Paul McCartney, George Harrison and Ringo Starr.

Benjamin Britten, 1913-1976, was a composer who wrote several famous operas, as well as songs, symphonies and choral music.

Charlie Chaplin, 1889-1977, was a film actor. He made many silent comedy films during the 1920s and 1930s.

Winston Churchill, 1874-1965, was a leading politician for over 50 years. As Prime Minister, he inspired the British during the Second World War (see page 27).

Winston Churchill

Eamon De Valera, 1882-1975, was a Republican leader during the Irish Civil War and was imprisoned by the British.

Edward Elgar, 1857-1934, was one of the greatest of English composers. He is best known for his Enigma Variations.

T.S. (Thomas Stearns) Eliot, 1888-1965, was a pioneer of modern poetry. Many critics hated his new and daring verse.

John ('Jackie') Fisher, 1841-1920, reformed the Royal Navy and built up a fleet of Dreadnoughts (see page 14).

Alexander Fleming, 1881-1955, was a Scottish doctor who discovered the important medicine penicillin in 1928.

Margot Fonteyn, 1919-1991, was Britain's leading ballerina for over 30 years. Her partnership with the Russian Rudolf Nureyev was world famous.

Barbara Hepworth, 1903-1975, was a sculptor. She worked in wood, stone and metal.

Amy Johnson, 1903-1941, was one of the first woman air pilots. She made many long solo flights, including one to Australia in 1930 (see page 22).

Amy Johnson

David Lloyd George, 1863-1945, was a Welsh politician who became Prime Minister during the First World War.

David Lloyd George

Henry Moore, 1898-1986, was the son of a miner who became a major modern sculptor. Some of his large works can be seen in parks and by public buildings.

Laurence Olivier, 1907-1989, was an actor on stage and in films. He was especially celebrated for his performances in the plays of Shakespeare.

George Orwell was the pen name of Eric Blair, 1903-1950. He wrote several fine novels, including *Animal Farm* and *Nineteen Eighty-Four*, a chilling look at the future.

Emmeline Pankhurst, 1858-1928, campaigned to win votes for women (see page 8).

Emmeline Pankhurst

Fred Perry, born 1909, was men's tennis champion at Wimbledon between 1934 and 1936 – the last Briton to achieve this. In 1929 he was world table-tennis champion.

Ernest Rutherford, 1871-1937, was a scientist from New Zealand who worked at Cambridge. He showed how atoms are made up of particles and was a pioneer of nuclear physics.

Ernest Shackleton, 1874-1922, was an Irish explorer. He made three trips to Antarctica, but never reached the South Pole.

Marie Stopes, 1880-1958, opened the first family planning clinic in London in 1921. Her work helped people to understand birth control much better.

Robert Watson-Watt, 1892-1973, was a Scottish scientist who invented radar. This played a vital part in detecting enemy bombers in the Second World War.

Frank Whittle, born 1907, developed the jet engine for aircraft. His first jet flew in 1941.

Virginia Woolf, 1882-1941, was a novelist. She tried new ways of writing fiction, in books such as *The Waves* and *To the Lighthouse*.

W.B. (William Butler) Yeats, 1865-1939, was the finest modern Irish poet. Many of his poems were inspired by love, or by Irish myths (see page 17).

THE 20TH-CENTURY ROYAL FAMILY TREE

This 'tree' shows the main 'branches' of the royal family leading up to Queen Elizabeth II and her family.

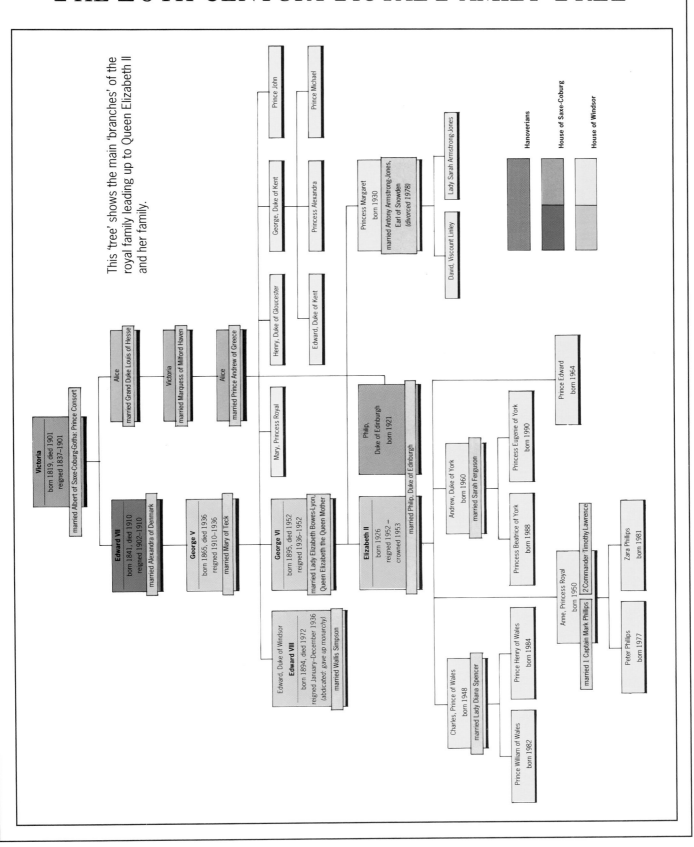

Legend:
- Hanoverians
- House of Saxe-Coburg
- House of Windsor

Victoria born 1819, died 1901, reigned 1837–1901 — married Albert of Saxe-Coburg-Gotha: Prince Consort

Alice — married Grand Duke Louis of Hesse

Victoria — married Marquess of Milford Haven

Alice — married Prince Andrew of Greece

Edward VII born 1841, died 1910, reigned 1902–1910 — married Alexandra of Denmark

George V born 1865, died 1936, reigned 1910–1936 — married Mary of Teck

Edward, Duke of Windsor **Edward VIII** born 1894, died 1972, reigned January–December 1936 (abdicated: gave up monarchy) — married Wallis Simpson

George VI born 1895, died 1952, reigned 1936–1952 — married Lady Elizabeth Bowes-Lyon, Queen Elizabeth the Queen Mother

Mary, Princess Royal

Philip, Duke of Edinburgh born 1921

Elizabeth II born 1926, reigned 1952 – crowned 1953 — married Philip, Duke of Edinburgh

Henry, Duke of Gloucester

Edward, Duke of Kent

Prince John

George, Duke of Kent

Princess Alexandra

Prince Michael

Princess Margaret born 1930 — married Antony Armstrong-Jones, Earl of Snowden (divorced 1978)

David, Viscount Linley

Lady Sarah Armstrong-Jones

Charles, Prince of Wales born 1948 — married Lady Diana Spencer

Prince William of Wales born 1982

Prince Henry of Wales born 1984

Anne, Princess Royal born 1950 — married 1 Captain Mark Phillips / 2 Commander Timothy Lawrence

Peter Phillips born 1977

Zara Phillips born 1981

Andrew, Duke of York born 1960 — married Sarah Ferguson

Princess Beatrice of York born 1988

Princess Eugenie of York born 1990

Prince Edward born 1964

GLOSSARY

airship an aircraft with a main body which is filled with a gas that is lighter than air, and which can be steered. A cabin beneath the main body can carry passengers or goods.

artillery large guns too big to carry, used in war.

assembly line a line of factory machines and workers which put together a product (such as a car) in a series of operations until it is completed.

Catholic someone who is a member of the Christian church ruled from Rome by the Pope.

communist a person who believes that all resources, goods and factories should be owned in common.

Conservative Party one of the two main political parties in Parliament. It supports private businesses and free enterprise.

dole state payments to the poor or unemployed.

fascist someone who believes in government by a dictator.

flying boat an aircraft which can land and take off on water.

gas mask a mask worn over the face to keep out poisonous gases.

general election a nationwide election for Members of Parliament.

gramophone an early form of record player, a type of music centre.

Home Guard a force of volunteers organized in Britain during the Second World War to fight any invasion.

Home Rule the freedom of a country to govern itself.

hovercraft an aircraft which travels just above the ground or sea on a cushion of air.

immigrant someone who comes to live in a country from abroad.

IRA abbreviation of Irish Republican Army, a military branch of Sinn Fein, which wants Ireland to break free of Britain. The Provisional IRA wants to expel the British from Northern Ireland.

jazz dance music developed by black performers in the USA which became popular during the 1920s.

Labour Party one of the two main political parties in Parliament since the 1930s. It represents the trade unions and workers.

land girls young women who volunteered to work on farms during the Second World War.

licence fee payment to the state which gives someone official permission to own or use something, such as a car or a radio.

mortgage a loan usually from a bank or building society, to help someone buy a property. If the borrower fails to pay back the loan, the lender gets the property.

package holiday a holiday in which all transport, meals and hotels are arranged by a travel company.

prefab a pre-fabricated (ready-made) house of simple design which can be built quickly.

Protestant a member of one of the Christian churches which split from the Catholic church in the 16th century. Protestants do not accept the leadership of the Pope.

republic a country ruled by a group of officials elected by the people, with no monarch.

Socialist Party a political party whose policy is that every person should share the ownership and control of industry and have equal wealth.

streamlined specially shaped to move fast through air or water.

suburb an area of housing built on the edge of a town.

textiles woven or knitted cloth.

trade union an organization of workers set up to discuss and try and agree with employers over conditions of pay, hours of work and unemployment benefits.

volunteer a person who offers their services or help, sometimes without payment or reward.

wireless an old name for a radio – something which receives and reproduces sounds without wires.

workhouse a place where poor people were given food and shelter in exchange for work.

Places to Visit

Here are some modern buildings and museums of modern interest to visit. Your local tourist office will be able to tell you about places in your area.

Barbican, London A complex of modern buildings, with houses, schools and theatre, built on an area bombed during the Second World War.

Canary Wharf, Docklands, London A giant office tower completed in 1991. It is well lit at night.

Channel Tunnel Entrance, Folkestone, Kent The brand-new rail link with France.

Chartwell, Westerham, Kent The home of Winston Churchill, with many records of his long life.

Coventry Cathedral, Coventry, Warwickshire Modern cathedral on the site of one destroyed by bombing in the Second World War.

Dolaucothi Gold Mines, Dyfed Underground tours of a mine that was still working until 1938.

Duxford Airfield, Cambridge The Imperial War Museum's collection of historic aircraft, from biplanes to Concorde.

Glasgow Museum of Transport, Glasgow Includes a fine display of modern ships.

Glasgow School of Art, Glasgow Completed in 1909, this is a beautiful modern building, with stained glass and metalwork.

Heathrow Airport Britain's main passenger and cargo aircraft terminal. There are aircraft viewing points for use by the general public.

HMS Belfast, London The largest surviving Second World War battleship, now moored on the Thames.

Imperial War Museum, London World War collections.

Leeds Industrial Museum, Yorkshire Includes a reconstructed 1920s cinema showing old films.

Letchworth, Hertfordshire The first 'Garden City' of 1903, a new town carefully planned and spacious, with trees and open spaces rather than factories and signs of industry.

Liverpool Cathedral, Merseyside A modern church building of concrete and glass.

Lloyd's Building, City of London A high-tech headquarters building, just right for the computer age.

Museum of Communication, Edinburgh A history of radio, telephones and other communications equipment.

Museum of Costume, Bath, Avon Includes a large collection of 20th-century clothes.

Museum of Flight, North Berwick, East Lothian Many historic aircraft, including an airship.

National Motor Museum, Beaulieu, Hampshire Tells the story of the motor car from 1894 to the present.

National Museum of Ireland, Dublin Has a section on the modern struggle for independence from Britain.

National Museum of Photography, Film and Television, Bradford, Yorkshire Exhibitions exploring the technology, art and craft of every type of camera.

Severn Bridge, Gloucestershire One of the longest suspension bridges in the world, linking England and Wales.

Ulster Museum, Belfast Includes a section on the 'troubles' of the early 20th century

Index